RONALD LAING

David Boyle is a co-director of the New Weather Institute, and the author of a number of books about economics, business and the future, as well as history, including *Blondel's Song* and *Toward the Setting Sun*, about the discovery of America. He is responsible for launching time banks in the UK and has stood for Parliament.

www.david-boyle.co.uk

Ronald Laing

The rise and fall and rise of a revolutionary psychiatrist

David Boyle

THE REAL PRESS
www.therealpress.co.uk

Published in 2016 by the Real Press.
www.therealpress.co.uk © David Boyle

ISBN (print) 978-0993523984
ISBN (ePub) 978-0993523991

"What is to be done? We who are still half alive, living in the often fibrillating heartland of a senescent capitalism — can we do more than reflect the decay around and within us? Can we do more than sing our sad and bitter songs of disillusion and defeat? The requirement of the present, the failure of the past, is the same: to provide a thoroughly self-conscious and self-critical human account of man."

R. D.Laing, *The Politics of Experience*, 1967

Contents

I

Introduction:
Events in inner space-time

"I am a specialist, God help me, in events in inner space and time."
R. D. Laing, 1964

It was a strange year, 1973. There was an energy crisis which destroyed the certainties of the postwar generation. Oil shot up in price. There was war in the Middle East. There were private armies in the UK, widespread industrial action and people like David Bowie singing about "five years – that's all we've got".

There was bombing, rioting and, by the end of the year, a three-day week enforced by law which forbade companies to work any more than that. And, amidst the chaos and the fundamental questions and criticisms, the world of psychiatry was rocked by a study published that year in *Science* by the Stanford

University professor, David Rosenhan.

Rosenhan had tested the assumptions of conventional psychiatric medicine to destruction by seeing how they stood up to the real world. He recruited a team of his students, including himself, who were all instructed to go to their doctor complaining of hearing voices in their head. It was the only symptom they would mention – they would otherwise have no problems or issues, mental or physical. The voices would say rather anodyne things like "thud". The pretend patients would have no previous mental issues either.

Without exception, Rosenhan's students all found themselves admitted to mental hospital, diagnosed with schizophrenia. Once they were in hospital, their instructions were all the same. They were to behave completely normally and they found their experience of incarceration was also remarkably similar. Not one of the fake patients was recognised as sane by the hospital staff and, over a period of between seven and 53 days, they were all discharged as "schizophrenics whose symptoms had temporarily abated".

Rosenhan was able to see the clinical notes written about his team when they were in hospital, and was fascinated to find that nothing they could do would be interpreted as sane. One of his stduents kept a diary about his time in hospital, and had been seen doing so by one of the hospital staff, who had written that "he indulges in writing behaviour". It was a telling, worrying phrase.

What he could not have hoped for when he was designing his experiment was what happened next. The research team had involved twelve mental hospitals, and they were not happy when the news came out with the publication of Rosenhan's study. But another one – what had not been involved – boasted in the public forore that followed that it would never happen there. Rosenhan seized the initiative and threatened to send some fake patients there too. The hospital then judged 41 of 193 recent patients as sane, and – only when he discovered this – Rosenhan revealed that he had actually not sent them any.

"It is clear that we cannot distinguish the sane from the insane in mental hospitals," Rosenhan wrote in the journal *Science*. The article had the title 'On being sane in insane places'. The Rosenhan experiment went to the heart of an issue in psychiatry in those days, a generation ago, when all professions were suddenly under scrutiny for the arrogant ways they used their professional privileges and powers. After all, psychiatrists could uniquely lock up people they decided were not sane, and do so indefinitely, without a second opinion, and carry out a series of irreversible and unproven treatments on them without their consent.

But what did it mean? These days we might call the phenomenon 'groupthink', the way elite groups of intelligent people are in the grip of an unquestioning method and language which seems immune to refutation or contradiction from the world outside. Rosenhan seemed to imply that psychiatry was in the grip of a series of self-supporting assumptions about the sanity or otherwise of the population, which had no obvious relationship to the real world.

But the most important implication was set out clearly by Rosenhan: it seemed to imply also that psychiatrists were unable to tell the sane from the insane, with serious implications for these concepts. It seemed to imply, if nothing else, that there was something seriously wrong with the whole mental health profession.

The Rosenhan experiment carried within it something of the spirit of the age. The Israeli doctors' strike that same year had unexpectedly led to a drop in mortality. The economist Fritz Schumacher had turned economic objectives inside out. The former Roman Catholic priest Ivan Ilich had famously done the same for schools and hospitals, and – at the time the most famous, not to say notorious of them all – R. D. Laing, had been doing the same for psychiatry.

In fact, Rosenhan had been inspired to try his experiment during a lecture by Laing about how insecure conventional psychiatric definitions were. He had wondered if he could design an experiment to test the proposition. It turned out that he could.

Ronald Laing was an enigma, a Scottish revolutionary psychiatrist at the height of his fame, and people immediately saw that Rosenhan's findings were important evidence that Laing was right. But exactly what Laing was saying was never entirely clear – was he saying that psychiatrists were not attached enough to the real world? Or was he going much further and questioning the existence of a distinction between sane and insane – questioning whether there was actually a real world at all? Was he claiming that psychiatrists were policing the boundaries between sanity and madness rather badly – or was he saying there was no such boundary?

The truth was that he veered between the two as part of a profound critique of modern life. There were certainly those who were sceptical about the whole idea of madness, as if it was entirely a socially constructed idea. As if society had got together and designated some behaviour mad because it was just too difficult to deal with – or maybe because living in an insane world sent some people over the edge. They were led by Laing's sometime friend David Cooper, who had dubbed his movement 'antipsychiatry'.

Laing always repudiated that label. What was quite clear was that Laing was at the heart of a passionate debate, and a bitter argument, about sanity and what it meant – and how to claw it back – which seemed to go to the very heart of everything. Especially when the world seemed pretty insane, was perched on the edge of nuclear oblivion, and seemed unable to heal the rifts between rich and poor, black and white, old and young and East and West. The mid-1970s were, in some ways, the most insane years to live through, which meant they were also a thrilling period of debate, when every assumption appeared to be open to challenge.

Since his groundbreaking book *A Divided Self* was published in a popular Penguin edition in 1965, Laing had been on a stratospheric journey that took him from a career as a major critic of the psychiatric establishment, and a spokesperson for those who had been misused by it, to something else entirely – a religious guru, the author of a million radical T-shirt slogans, a leading poet, a social critic and a theological maverick.

The final lines of his 1967 book *The Bird of Paradise* had included the famous lines: "If I could turn you on, if I drive you out of your wretched mind, if I could tell you, I would let you know".

The message was somewhat obscure but it appealed to the hippy spirit. There was something about the words which implied Laing was struggling to communicate something, perhaps even struggling to understand something vital about life and our combined human future, that he was not yet able to get across. It implied that the great existentialist psychiatrist was being held back in some way because the very language was so restricting. No wonder he had moved on to writing poetry.

Certainly, his precise message was never quite pinned down. Sometimes he was quiet and respectful, just asking pinpointed and challenging questions of an unthinking elite, and by implication a boneheaded establishment behind them. Sometimes he was offering opinions on how we might live, appearing drunk or drugged on stage, and leading a radical movement that included the other great gurus of the age, Marcuse, Fanon or Sartre.

In fact, their names were bracketed with his in the Fontana 'Modern Masters' series published at the time. He was an enigma. It is now nearly three decades since his early death at the age of 61, and he is as much of an enigma as ever.

It is even longer, nearly half a century, since Rosenhan's research which marked the high point of Laing's fame. His fame has declined but his influence can still be seen everywhere. There are hardly any mental hospitals left, partly the result of an effective campaign led by Laing's contemporary radical psychiatrist, Franco Basaglia, who was horrified by what he found in Italian asylums after being appointed to the one in Gorizia.

In other ways, the situation has barely improved. Treatments are often a good deal more effective and more permanent than those offered in Laing's day. Mental hospital inmates are no longer treated with quite the patronising disdain, and sheer cruelty, that Laing and Basaglia exposed to the light of day. But those in great mental distress are often forced to beg for help from overstretched mental health trusts, or to live isolated lives being cared for 'in the community', which tends to mean not being cared for at all. Those in the grip of mental ill-health – which may be anything up to a quarter of us at some time in our lives – are categorised against the same kind of numerical classifications that Laing condemned, and weaned onto drugs that can still undermine their ability to recover.

In other, deeper ways, the ideas and the

intellectual tradition that Laing represented – a revolt against over-rational, one-dimensional approaches to attempt to rule us – have been sidelined into the 'alternative' by a powerfully resurgent technocracy. His appeal to authentic living remains influential, but tends to fall victim to cynics, technocrats and marketers alike.

Laing was deeply influenced by Jean-Paul Sartre and the European existentialists, and borrowed from their interpretation of mental illness. Existential psychiatry was not about restoring patients to an acceptable level of sanity; it was about restoring them to themselves. It was a subjective, self-validating process that he believed constituted real healing. Since his death, we have been all but overwhelmed by a different idea of technocratic healing, categorising, providing specified treatments, an objective process mediated by drugs and ratified by professionals.

Laing's was a platonist approach, which spread in the thrilling ferment of the time to medicine, education and child rearing – and it implied that we carried the seeds of sanity, or health or wisdom within us, and the task of the professional is not to standardise us but to help us draw it out.

But the spirit of 1973 was not to last. The age to come would reject ideas like this, and it has steamrollered over existential psychiatry, complementary health and alternative education.

This book tells Laing's story as a way of looking at this peculiar period of recent history, and as a way of looking at the intellectual revolt that seems largely now over. But most of all, it tells the story of the questions Laing asked his fellow psychiatrists, sometimes with devastating results – and the experiments he tested out with varying degrees of success – and of a man with a unique ability to empathise with his patients, rising in a profession that disapproved of anything of the kind.

Above all, it is a story of a human being who believed that human empathy had a critical role in the process of change. Because, as we will see – change and its possibilities and facilitation were the ideas that obsessed Laing and why he remains a great mind of the twentieth century.

Towards the end of his life, Laing wrote his own autobiography, *Wisdom, Madness and Folly*. He told the story up to the publication of *A Divided Self* which first catapulted him to such fame and notoriety. He deliberately flung the spotlight primarily onto the great mental struggle that he had forced himself to go through to identify the discomfort that was gnawing away at him about his own profession.

"The situation keeps cropping up in our society when, no matter how liked, esteemed or loved, some people become insufferable to others," wrote Laing then. "No-one they know wants to live with them, they are not breaking the law, but they arouse in those around them such urgent feelings of pity, worry, fear, disgust, anger, concern, exasperation, that something has to be done."

That was the original problem that he worried away at. There was something about the power he was being asked to wield over these people that worried him so much that he could not let it go. "Within two years of carrying out my duties as a clinical psychiatrist," he wrote, "I came to the painful realisation that I would not like to be treated the way my own patients had to be treated."

This required a leap of imagination that was clearly not possible for so many of his fellow professionals, who had become used to considering mental patients as an 'other' that they barely needed to communicate with. But then Laing was always sensitive, sometimes acutely sensitive, to the feelings and needs of his patients. Often he seemed more at ease with people in great mental distress than he was with the comfortable middle classes who craved his challenging words of wisdom. He was so uniquely sensitive to the misery of the world, as he saw it, and he felt it as a crushing force, in a way that most of us cannot bear to. It was Laing who realised that, often, being with someone in distress can be healing in itself – just treating them as human beings.

It was this realisation that made him fear that some of this overwhelming misery was "being manufactured by psychiatry itself". That revelation, and human pity and its power to heal and ability to make change happen, is why Laing remains important to this day, and why the story I am about to tell still has the power to move.

II
The realisation

*"The term schizoid refers to an individual the
totality of whose experience is split in two main
ways: in the first place, there is a rent in his
relationship with the world and, in the second, there
is a disruption of his relation with himself."*

R. D. Laing,
the opening lines of *A Divided Self*

Ronald Laing was born in October 1927, in a
tenement in the Glasgow neighbourhood of
Govanhill. His father David had been a naval
architect – in the days when the River Clyde
produced so much of the world's shipping – but he
had a nervous breakdown in his fifties and turned to
drink and aggression. David Laing swore he had no
idea how his wife Amelia got pregnant after nine
years of marriage, since absolutely no sex was taking
place. This is not such a rare phenomenon as it

seems. Ronald always claimed he could remember hearing his father singing when he was in the womb, and that he remembered being born, and the snip of the scissors that cut his umbilical cord. He was always fascinated by memories of birth. He was named after the film star Ronald Colman.

The story of the virgin birth implies a peculiarity in the relationship between Laing's parents, and there certainly was, but there was a formative peculiarity in particular in his relationship with his mother. Amelia Laing was isolated and isolating, and she was deeply jealous of anything or anyone else that the young Ronald loved. She smashed his beloved baby grand piano with an axe because he was too fond of it. She forbade him from seeing his aunt because he was getting to care about her – and finally, as an adult, she began sticking pins into an effigy of him after she saw the word 'fuck' in his 1967 book *The Politics of Experience*.

The tension increased as he got old enough to resist her bullying. He developed eczema at the age of five and then asthma. In later life, Laing used to tell two revealing stories about his relationship with his mother. The first happened at the age of seven, when she accused him of stealing a missing pen. She told his father he had confessed to it – perhaps to save him from being punished as a liar as well. If that was the reason, it was hardly effective, because Ronald still refused to admit it so he was beaten for stealing and lying too. At this point, he began to wonder if he had in fact stolen the pen. When it eventually turned up, and it was clear it had not been stolen after all, his mother said: "Come and kiss Mummy and make up."

But he refused to. He was still cross.

"Well, if you don't love your mummy, I'll just have to go away," she said. Laing described this later as a feeling of "terrifying deliverance".

The second incident ended with a real victory. He was never allowed to lock the bathroom door so that his mother could come in while he was in the bath and scrub his back. At the age of fourteen or fifteen, he locked the door. There was a terrible commotion until finally his father had to drag his mother away by force. It proved to be the moment that Amelia Laing convinced herself of her son's inherent wickedness.

They had no visitors and his mother never went out. When she went into hospital for a gallbladder operation, she refused to tell the medical staff anything about herself, even her address.

"Don't you realise, your mother's mad?" the neurosurgeon Joe Schorstein, his mentor, told him later. Laing was surprised.

His father had his difficulties too. In fact, Laing used to describe his father as his first patient, because of the long conversations they had after his father found himself trembling uncontrollably.

Laing's career as a contrarian may have begun from the moment he and another pupil walked out of school in protest at the idea of using film of concentration camps as a teaching aid. The idea of studying music – he played the piano – was delayed by breaking his wrist, so he decided on medicine at Glasgow University. He then found himself increasingly fascinated by psychiatry, from watching the hypnotic power of Billy Graham's evangelism – and reading an article in *Horizon* magazine by the French playwright Antonin Artaud, who had spent some time in an asylum against his will in the south of France.

Laing was becoming drawn to the idea of unpalatable truths, and sympathised with people in mental distress because they were doing the same. "A lunatic is a man society does not wish to listen to and whom it is determined to prevent from uttering unbearable truths," wrote Laing. It was a point of view of mental health which had Vincent Van Gogh as its patron saint.

There was a telling moment while he was a medical student when a hideously deformed baby, more like a frog than a human being, was born dead. Laing had wrapped it up and taken it with him to a bar on the way home, and felt a powerful temptation – which he resisted – to unwrap it and confront people with it, as the real truth about the horrors underneath human life that they preferred to insulate themselves against. Which, after all, was the sanest approach – the need to tell the truth or the need to avoid it?

"It began to be clear to me that I was involved with the puzzle of human misery," he wrote later. "And one of the things that deeply disturbed and puzzled me was why the world we live in was such a miserable, cruel and violent place."

Laing graduated from Glasgow University in 1951, and was sent to a neurosurgical unit at Killearn near Loch Lomond, where he had to assist during long, intricate brain operations, shining torches into brain cavities. He passed out twice. He was initially torn between the mysteries of the brain and the mysteries of the mind, but was fascinated more by the latter – Laing was always aware that the workings of the human mind always seem to break out of the neat categories we prepare for them.

He thought a great deal about the case of a girl thrown from a horse who stayed concussed for four days, but imitated the horse while she was unconscious. There was no explanation for that which you could find in a brain cavity, after all.

The Korean War was in full spate and Laing was called up. He lay on his bed training to be an officer in an army psychiatric unit, reading existentialist philosophy. It wasn't the training the army quite had in mind.

Being called up and posted to the Royal Army Medical Corps unit at Netley, rather than to study with the eminent Swiss psychologist Karl Jaspers, where he wanted to go, was a huge disappointment. But like so often in people's lives, it was a disappointment that plunged him into the experience which, more than any other, was to shape his career as a maverick. Because, if you wanted to choose the one place in Britain where psychiatry had most become a caricature of itself, it was the place he was sent.

Netley was in many ways a conventional psychiatric unit, which used the theories of the Italian psychiatrist Ugo Cerletti, a professor at Rome University, primarily known because he had designed snow camouflage for the Italian army during the First World War. Perhaps it was Cerletti's military background which appealed to the officers at

Netley, but Cerletti had claimed that epilepsy and schizophrenia were the opposites of each other. It made sense, or so the theory went, that to escape one, you had to induce the other.

Netley therefore had an insulin ward of twenty beds, where patients were deliberately put into an insulin coma and the staff walked around in the dark with torches. The danger was that this would actually induce epileptic fits. It was an extremely dangerous procedure, but justified somehow because it was supposed to be in the interests of the patient.

This was explained partly by the fact that there was an important difference between Netley and a civilian psychiatric department. It was a military unit, which explained why they were able easily to believe an epileptic seizure which might kill them was, at least, for their own good. The main focus wasn't necessarily the good of the patients. The main questions which this particular establishment wrestled with were: how and in what circumstances could these patients be discharged from military life? Were they actually faking to get out of the army or to avoid frontline duties? Or did you have to be crazy *not* to want to leave, as in the novel *Catch-22*.

This last question was one that, rather unexpectedly, went to the heart of Laing's work, and he became fascinated with it. How could you tell the sane from the insane? In other branches of medicine, you could look at red or white blood cells or other telltale signs under a microscope, but in psychiatry you usually couldn't.

In practice, the army was trying to weed out the malingerers by making their experience of insanity so unpleasant that they preferred not to be there. In practice, Laing found that most of his patients – the sane and the insane – were far too shattered to have managed the experience of war.

What increasingly worried Laing were the standing methods of dealing with patients in the unit. The treatments seemed to be a horrible bundle of hit or miss techniques, including Electro-Convulsive Therapy (ECT) or insulin comas, which may or may not make a difference, but would certainly quieten patients and make them easier to process. The whole purpose seemed to be to deaden the mind, because this was an institution – perhaps more than others he saw later – that was run partly for the benefit of the staff, and partly for the benefit of the army. And the staff clearly believed that, once a diagnosis had been lifted from the list and applied, no further progress or understanding could be made. That was it. Netley was a machine for categorisation not for cure.

But that wasn't quite the worst of it. There was

also the doctrine of silence which was taken particularly seriously at Netley. It was believed at the time that schizophrenics should be kept isolated from human communication. There were strict instructions not to talk to patients and, if they were seen talking to each other, the staff were expected to intervene quickly to break it up. Talking was supposed to make psychosis worse.

There were occasional successes with the induced coma treatment, but there were also occasional deaths. But the rest of those cared for at Netley were reduced to this isolated, sub-human existence, without human contact or conversation or kindness. It was not designed to foster sanity.

"You must not let a schizophrenic talk to you," Laing explained their attitude. "It aggravates the psychotic process."

Part of the problem was that Laing himself felt separate from the whole process and confused. His training suggested one thing; his conscience and his intuition suggested something else. Writing *A Divided Self* some years later, he admitted to "personal difficulties I have in being a psychiatrist". All too often, he found he was unable to see the signs and symptoms of psychosis that those around were seeing. "I used to think that this was some deficiency on my part, that I was not clever enough to get at hallucinations and delusions and so on." He could not see what the text books said he should be able to see. Was he stupid? Or was he perhaps suffering from some kind of psychosis himself? He wasn't absolutely sure.

But the injunction not to communicate with patients was a real struggle. Was it for their good, after all, or was it actually for the good of the staff? And how was he supposed to find out anything about his patients if he didn't interact with them on a reasonably equal basis? He began to sit in cells with them, staying quiet and listening and watching, always in the guise of research.

The most notorious incident followed his questioning of patients. One of them had what he described later as an interesting hallucination. He dreamed he had been dragged out of bed in the middle of the night while he was drugged with insulin and beaten by people in army uniform. When the second patient came up with the same dream, it was a fascinating coincidence. When four of them came up with the same story, it was clear that something was seriously wrong. As a result, a corporal and a private were court martialled and given two years hard labour.

Though Laing did not describe this as a clue, that is what it was. The phenomenon has been all too common throughout human history, from the conquistadors to Huntingdon Life Science. When cruelties are permitted on people or animals, it seems to lead to active dislike among those charged with their care. And there was now no doubt in Laing's mind that the system of military psychiatry, organised as it was for the good of the army, meant that the cruelties of lobotomies and electric shock treatments got in the way of the human connection. He wouldn't want to be treated in that way if their roles were reversed and he was the patient. He felt he could no longer in all conscience flick the switch to turn on the electric current.

"It was not easy to retain this feeling when I pressed the button to give someone an electric shock," he wrote, "if I could not feel I was doing to him what I hoped he would do for me if I had his brains and he mine. I gave up pressing the button."

It was an encounter with an eighteen-year-old patient who was raving that gave Laing the insight he needed. The patient he called 'John' in *Self and Others* was disturbed in his cell in the middle of the night. Laing went to get an injection to calm him down, but it wasn't necessary. He sat with him without consciously trying to make sense of his fantasies about being a cat burglar. After that encounter, Laing got into the habit of taking refuge in John's cell and listening to him. He found just listening to him calmed John down without an injection.

He became fascinated with John, who had been disowned and forced into the army by his father when he failed his university entrance. John was, in short, someone who had been impelled to create his own identity. He later recovered and was discharged, but there was more than a sense in which Laing had accompanied him on parts of his journey.

"When I started to meet psychotic patients professionally, I found, to my alarm, that sometimes I could see their point of view all too well," he wrote later. "If I didn't wish to ruin my career, I would have to be very circumspect." Here was the power of professional psychiatry. If you saw things differently to them, you didn't just disagree – you began to wonder about your own sanity. That was clearly something that Laing did all too frequently throughout his career.

There was a moment with a patient of his called Peter when Laing realised he could not go home for a week to Glasgow, knowing that Peter might be taken for ECT while he was away and unable to veto the idea.

So on an impulse, he took Peter along with him. He stayed curled up in his room for three days. "Any ordinary psychiatrist would have had him admitted right away. But the other side of me, the ordinary human being who found himself at the beginning of a psychiatric career, would have felt that to do so would have been to betray him completely."

Peter also recovered but it wasn't clear to Laing until later what this meant for his career, and what a maverick he was becoming. For the time being, he was still firmly in the mainstream, promoted to captain and posted to the Catterick Military Hospital. It was there that he heard from a nursing sister at Netley, Anne Hearne, that she was six months pregnant. After agonising about his on-off romance in France, he married her in October 1952. Neither of his parents came to the wedding.

Catterick was a "palace of misery, absurdity and humiliation", he wrote later. Safe in his room in the officer's quarters, he imagined the barracks and detention wards, across the parade ground, as places of groans and tears.

When Laing was discharged from the army in 1953, he was given a job at the Gartnavel Royal Mental Hospital in Glasgow, where he needed to go to finish his psychiatric training. He moved there with Anne and his first daughter, Fiona.

What he found at Gartnavel was a kind of mental health class system. There were patients in relative comfort who paid fees and got single rooms, and the rest who were crammed into a ward and saw a doctor once every six months. They were allowed no personal possessions. Some had been there for as long as 60 years.

It was the first time Laing had been responsible for women mental patients and he was fascinated. Aware of the arms-length regime the psychiatrists had put in place to keep their patients at a distance, he decided to stay nights on the ward. The first night he did so, the women had tried to take his trousers off, and he had to be rescued by the staff. Later, they came to accept him being there and left him alone.

But he became aware, talking to some of the patients in their more lucid periods, that some of them could provide far better insights into their friends on the ward than the staff could. He began to wonder how much it was the intensely regimented regime which was making them behave in such an autistic or self-absorbed way.

The thing was that psychiatric hospitals were regimented places. They had to be – big institutions have to be regimented if they are going to avoid chaos. The question was whether it was possible to heal people in their minds in such an inhumane environment. Laing was coming to believe that people had a natural rhythm of life and felt that interfering with it could prevent recovery – but what could you do?

Well, he could see if it might be possible to blunt some of the excesses. One of his first experiments at Garnavel was simply to find out the effects on the patients of being locked in. In one ward, he reduced the drugs to practically zero and locked the door. In the first week of the experiment, about 30 windows were smashed. Nobody was hurt, so from the second week onwards, he unlocked the doors and found there was no rush to leave, and the windows stayed intact. It wasn't that the patients were desperate to escape. They just hated being locked in.

None of these experiments went down well with the psychiatric staff, but in his mind, Laing was building up a series of overwhelming questions with which he was interrogating conventional psychiatry. He found that, when you probed with small, simple experiments, his patients did not react in the way the conventional model assumed. In fact, they reacted rather as human beings were supposed to react.

None of this was without its complications, or its opposition or the doubts that the experiments sowed in his own mind, but it was all building up into a different way of understanding mental distress and schizophrenia in particular.

But as they had in Netley, it was the patients themselves who surprised him and broke out of the neat categories in which they had been put. One of these was known as Phillip, who Laing became responsible for when he moved to his next posting. Phillip had gone through experiences which might have broken anyone. He had found his mother dead in a pool of blood from tuberculosis. Then he had been forced to endure his father's rages every day, accusing him of causing her death, only to find him hanging from a hook in the living room two months later.

Six months after that, Phillip had sunk into a complete self-absorption, had a terrible stutter on the rare occasions that he spoke, and was doubly incontinent. Nobody wanted him in the world outside, and the ward staff wanted him out of there. He smelled appalling. He was the very definition of an acute catatonic schizophrenic.

Laing interviewed Phillip alone, and asked him if he would like to take a seat. To his astonishment, Phillip sat down politely and began to explain "where he was at". It transpired that he was spending his time thinking about the mysteries of calculus.

Because of this surprising revelation, Laing carried on the interview, ignoring the smell and talking to Phillip every day, and he felt that this attitude of polite benevolence did seem to be getting through. He was talking more and much calmer, at least in Laing's office. After six weeks, Laing took the huge risk of discharging Phillip and taking him to stay in his own home, where his wife Anne treated him with the same kind of humanity. His incontinence stopped immediately and – three months later – he was well enough to go on to another family. Laing ran into Phillip again fifteen years later, and he was married with a family of his own and taking evening classes in psychology.

The problem was that Laing's colleagues, psychiatrists and psychologists alike, seemed unable to step out of the role they were playing long enough to respond authentically as a human being, or so it seemed to Laing. As a bare minimum, they would insist on interpreting every gesture within the psychological rules of the game. Like asking for a glass of water.

What would he do if a patient asked him for one, he was asked by a group of psychologists in the 1980s?

"I would give him or her a glass of water and sit down in my chair again," he replied.

"You would not make an interpretation?"

One woman then said: "I'm totally lost!"

Perhaps the problem was that the professionals just needed a dose of real life. Like economists, Laing felt that psychiatrists had cut themselves off from the way people really behaved.

When he moved on from Gartnavel, he was given the job of senior registrar in Glasgow at the Southern General Hospital, the youngest in the country in that role. The man who was most instrumental in the appointment was his new boss, Angus MacNiven, a vigorous opponent of ECT, and well-known for his habit of talking to patients.

It so happened, in 1955, that the psychology department at Southern General was asked by a group of religious leaders in Glasgow if they could be given a course in human relationships. There were seven protestant ministers and a rabbi, and it was clear to Laing that actually the education was going the other way around. The ministers had experience of the way people behaved in the real world and some of it bore little relation to the text books.

It was supposed to be sane to feel grief when a partner died, but the ministers all agreed that people often felt a sense of liberation, or a range of other emotions. If sanity did not relate to the textbook definitions, then how could insanity? "I realised how little I knew of real life," he wrote later.

But the experiment that would come to define Laing's career had taken place within three months of him first arriving in Gartnavel, back in 1953. It was what had convinced him, more than anything else, that treating mental patients a little more like human beings might speed along their recovery – because he had begun to suspect that there may have been an element of schizophrenia that was a healing process. Stop the process by giving the sufferers powerful electric shocks or just by treating them like sub-humans, and withdrawing human sympathy or contact, and you threatened to atrophy them in their withdrawn state. But the Rumpus Room experiment would dramatise the issues, and these interpretations would come later.

Laing had asked his superiors if he could have a bright, spacious and comfortable room for twelve most intractable chronic patients. They would spend every day there from nine to five and have access to magazines, or rugmaking, allowed to wear shoes, underwear and stockings and have their hair done. He also chose the twelve least popular patients, on the condition that none of them had been stuck by lobotomies or ECT. They were allowed to dress as they liked, like the staff, and to wear make-up. It was to be as normal as possible. Laing described the experience of watching the delight on their faces when they returned to the room for the second day, the next morning.

It came to be called the Rumpus Room. Two nurses were available all the time to give individual attention if the patients wanted it. In fact, the nurses became fond of their patients, and were accused by their overstretched colleagues of being unprofessional as a result.

The Rumpus Room was soon equipped with a gas hob and an oven and the patients cooked their own food. On one occasion, one of the doctors brought trays of buns made by the women to the psychiatrists' lounge. Most refused to touch them. "This incident convinced me of something," wrote Laing. "Who was crazier? Staff to patient excommunication runs deep. A companion means, literally, one with whom one shares bread. Companionship between staff and patients had broken down. The psychiatrists were afraid of catching schizophrenia."

Companionship and the lack of it, and the way that psychiatrists deliberately failed to provide it, were growing in importance for Laing. He could see there was something vitally human about it, and that was what seemed to give it a healing quality. The Rumpus Room experiment would carry a lot of weight for a range of ideas, but – at its root – it was about companionship and its place in a sane world.

To Laing and those who were now fascinated by him, and these would grow in number over the next two decades, the Rumpus Room was a huge success. It certainly influenced the future direction of Laing's career, but it wasn't an unambiguous success. Within 18 months, every patient in the room – previously deeply withdrawn – had been discharged from hospital. But within another year, they were all back again.

This simply exacerbated the divide between the radicals and conventional opinion. Was their return to hospital some kind of proof that schizophrenia was incurable after all, as Laing's colleagues maintained? Or was there, he wondered, also something about the basic insanity of the environment they went back to?

Because the whole structure of psychiatry, as practiced then, seemed to be dedicated to denying the patients this sense of solidarity. When he sat next to patients in distress, saying nothing, it was an act of communion with them which seemed to say that someone cared – and as a human equal. It was impossible in the psychiatric hospitals where he had worked so far. It may also have been impossible in their home environments, because of the kind of doublethink that Laing knew so well in his own upbringing that made human communion so tough.

The real problem, he felt, was that there was a huge and almost unbreachable divide between psychiatrists and their patients. It was a divide which meant there could be no communication, no communion across it and it was exacerbated by the way that it was the psychiatrists, not those in their care, who were often alienated – treating their patients in the most inhumane ways, giving them electric shocks for their own good because the progress of psychiatric opinion believed it had some effect to calm them – though there was little evidence that it would lead to any kind of recovery. Perhaps, he wondered, human contact was the best kind of treatment you could provide, giving a sense of solidarity – to be with them as they went through the *process* that schizophrenia represented.

That was going rather further than anything the Rumpus Room provided evidence for. But Laing had been reading the existentialist philosophers since before he was called up. He was steeped in the idea of alienation – not from the world outside, but from their true selves. His approach was coming to mean that schizophrenia or psychosis might be better understood – not as inconvenient symptoms of insanity – but as the way people maintained their existential integrity.

That meant that the authenticity of the physician was the key to healing. It meant that the psychiatrist's response must be real. It also meant that every psychosis was going to be an individual affair, and trying to assess or categorise it was an aggressive threat to that individuality and its authenticity.

Later, Laing and his colleagues would begin to apply these ideas to society, and to try – without being too political – to apply it to a critique of modern life, in an insane world which was designed to manufacture misery, and to designate assessment as a political and disempowering act. The big issue that was to emerge over the next decade was what this meant for us all – and how to become ourselves despite these insane pressures. Especially since the 1980s when there were those who wanted us to believe that external, economic pressures *were* the only reality.

But for now, it was the memory of the Rumpus Room and his suffering patients who drove Laing on. Politics and culture were for the future.

III
The rise...

"No age has so lost touch its natural healing process."
R. D. Laing, *Sanity, Madness and the Family*

His colleagues at Gartnavel had been fascinated by the experiment with the Rumpus Room but ruled out anything like it again. They were also unnerved by Laing's habit of sitting in an armchair to talk to patients rather than sitting behind a desk to defend the profession's dignity and authority.

It was when he discovered that, without asking him, some of his colleagues were working on a book using some of the Rumpus material that he realised he would have to do so himself. The young writer Colin Wilson had just published a huge bestseller called *The Outsider*, which drew on the European existentialist philosophy which also fascinated Laing, and which was in a way a foretaste of the 1960s social revolt against convention. Laing started writing the book that would come to be *The Divided Self* and tried to convey something of what it felt like to be mad.

Then and later, Laing was particularly influenced by the great German existentialist theologian Paul Tillich, living in exile from the Nazis in the USA, and his concept of 'ontological insecurity'. It was Tillich who also provided the main inspiration for Bishop John Robinson's controversial book *Honest to God*, which the purity campaigner Mary Whitehouse later pinpointed as the prime cause of the permissive society.

In fact, when Laing sent an article he had written about Tillich and mental illness to the *Journal of Medical Psychology*, it came to the notice of the highly respected Tavistock Clinic in London, because the editor was also medical director there. As a result, Laing was asked to come to London as senior registrar. He came with Anne and his burgeoning family and set up home in Harlow new town. Laing had attracted the interest of the psychological establishment and they wanted to employ him.

This meant he would have to qualify as a practicing psychotherapist. But he attended almost none of the seminars, because he had been furiously working away at his book, and the examination committee tried to hold him back a year. Some of the big names in psychology complained, D. W. Winnicott, Charles Rycroft and others, because of what they called his "challenging originality" and, as a result, he graduated in that year, 1960, after all.

The Tavistock was a bit of a disappointment to Laing. The patients were mainly white middle class and, as he wrote later, "none of them particularly disturbed". Also his book was turned down by six publishers and was eventually put out by Tavistock Publications, the in-house publishing arm, where it sold only 1,400 copies in four years.

Having qualified as a psychotherapist, he set up in practice at 21 Wimpole Street. But he was also beginning to experiment with taking hallucinogenic drugs like LSD, which was still legal at the time, fascinated by the way that allowed him to relive experiences from a long way back. His interest in the idea began in 1954 when he had read Aldous Huxley's book *The Doors of Perception*. His first LSD trip was as early as 1960, and thanks to his doctor friend Richard Gelfer.

He began to experiment with it in his practice. When he went to the USA four years later he was to link up with the future prophets of the psychedelic age, including Timothy Leary who had just been sacked from Harvard University for his LSD experiments.

At the same time, Laing was developing a story about modern life which regards most people as alienated from their true selves, partly because we have to adjust to a workload and social mores which are pretty insane. He believed we usually manage to adjust to the insanity by the age of fifteen. Ten years later, it is hard to remember anything – or so Laing believed – from what we have lost in the process of apparent civilisation. In fact, from the age of 25, we are largely estranged from our real, inner life: "Gone is any sense of tragedy, or passion," he wrote. "Gone is any language of joy, delight, passion, sex, violence. The language is that of the boardroom."

Laing was a hypnotic talker and sometimes a thrilling speaker: at the height of his fame, he attracted 4,000 people to hear him speak in Santa Monica, a week after Bob Dylan attracted the same number. One radio journalist described him as 'the white Martin Luther King'. People talked about his hypnotic eyes and his obscurity too. He was exciting and difficult to understand, but people felt a sense that Laing, alone among his colleagues, was touching a difficult and elusive truth – not just about mental illness, but about life.

While he was feeling frustrated at the Tavistock, his colleagues were also feeling frustrated with him. They didn't like his increasingly trenchant positions, nor his worryingly open personality, or the way he wept openly at the funerals of friends or at a performance of *Oh, What a Lovely War!,* Joan Littlewood's production which caught the spirit of the times by pinning the blame on Haig and his generals for the slaughter of the trenches. It was a play which spoke also to that sense, that Laing always conveyed, of being able to touch the despair and misery at the heart of existence more than the rest of us. It may have been one reason why he had such a following among people who were experiencing more intense despair than they needed to.

When the *British Journal of Psychiatry* turned down his polemic about the genetic theory of schizophrenia, it was the last straw. He left the Tavistock Clinic in 1962, and leading psychologists like John Bowlby dated this as the moment when he put himself deliberately outside the profession. Instead, he began to pursue the life of a pundit and inspiring guru, just at the moment that the mass media had made such an existence a possibility. Two years later, and even before his book had been widely read, he began appearing regularly on television. He gave a lecture at the Institute of Contemporary Arts in 1964, which began like this:

"From the moment of birth, when the Stone Age baby first confronts the twentieth century mother, the baby is subjected to these forces of outrageous violence, called love."

It was vintage Laing, able in one sentence to invert the accepted order of things, and to appeal to the sense of the violent, wildness at the heart of human life. There is even a hint in there that a mother's love can be destructive – which is certainly something he felt about his own upbringing. It was revolutionary and thrilling and it touched a truth which, in a sense, had been hidden until these liberated moments. The world was changing and Laing was positioning himself, perhaps unconsciously, as one of the forces that was changing it.

It was in response to his growing fame that Penguin Books decided to publish their mass market edition of *A Divided Self*. The book emerged as a Pelican in 1965, and finally reached a wider public. Laing was increasingly busy, writing, seeing patients, lecturing, appearing in the media. He had prodigious energy, not just for this but also for his experiments with hallucinogenics. It is hardly surprising that his family life began to suffer.

By 1965, his relationship with Anne had largely unravelled. He now had five children aged from three to nine and was rarely at home. Trying to decide what to do, he convened a council of male friends. One said that it would be unthinkable to leave five children. He took no notice, left anyway, and it was only after he came back from his 1972 visit to India that he tried to remake the links with his first family. He went on to have five more children.

Laing was at the heart of a shift in the way people understood what was important.

The poet Philip Larkin – whose famous poem "they fuck you up, your mum and dad" spoke to the movement that Laing represented – claimed that the world changed in 1963. But those of us who were there might reply that it was actually 1965. Or to be more precise, that was the year when pressure for change had built up such a force behind it that the dam broke. It was the year when the old world departed – which saw the deaths of T. S. Eliot, Winston Churchill and Stan Laurel. In the UK, 1965 was the year that the critic Kenneth Tynan first used the word 'fuck' on television.

A new spirit of informality and tolerance had burst against the stultifying conformity of the 1950s and the result was a great flowering of culture and confusion. It was the year of *The Killing of Sister George,* of *The Magic Roundabout,* of the Beatles film *Help!,* of Jacqueline du Pre's monumental performance of Elgar's Cello Concerto. It was a year to be alive.

One of the side-effects of this emerging revolt was that everyone, in their own way, seemed to feel like something of an outsider. It meant that Laing was suddenly providing the intellectual underpinning to a much wider movement for change. People didn't just have divided selves in mental hospitals, after all, but there was a sense in which a growing number of people felt alienated from those parts of themselves which had been constrained by social mores, or perhaps by economics.

Abortion was legalised in 1967, Homosexuality was legalised in 1969. The death penalty was abolished in 1965. The voluntary sector began to emerge as a vociferous element in national debate. There were adventure playgrounds, encounter groups, homelessness campaigns, city farms, peace campaigns, folk music concerts – and behind it all was this perhaps unacknowledged *platonism*, a sense that reality lay elsewhere – behind the social and economic mask, where there was a reality from which we had been estranged.

This was the debate and the raging spirit of the times of which Laing was finding himself one presiding genius. He was soon attracting disciples, followers and fellow travellers heading in similar, if not quite the same, directions. One of them was the South African psychiatrist David Cooper, who was working on his own book *The Death of the Family* (1971) and who coined the 'anti-psychiatry' phrase that would give Laing a good deal of trouble as he tried to define his constantly shifting position. Laing always denied he was an 'anti-psychiatrist'. He remained a psychiatrist for most of the rest of his life, insisting on his right to speak for mainstream psychiatry. In the end, it was the profession which kicked him out and not the other way round.

On the other hand, his thinking was becoming close to that of the radicals. The introduction to the Penguin edition of *A Divided Self* included a troublesome phrase which revealed just how far he had travelled, and would come back to haunt him. In the new preface, he wrote: "No-one can deny us the right to disbelieve in the fact of psychiatry".

There was the difficulty in a nutshell. What did Laing think schizophrenia was? Was mental illness just the way society labelled those it couldn't stand? Was schizophrenia just some kind of social construct, which did not really exist? In which case, why did it cause so much distress and pain? Was there no real task that psychiatrists could reasonably carry out? Later, Laing would row back from some of these ideas, aware that the pain that schizophrenics were going through was absolutely real. But if schizophrenia was a real phenomenon, what was it exactly? Even back at Netley Baracks and Catterick, when he was still in the army, Laing had begun to wonder whether it was playing some other role than irritation and misery.

Maybe there was some healing role that schizophrenia was playing, as some physical ailments do. The complete suppression of the symptoms, to the extent of removing part of the brain, was not then going to do anything except freeze the schizophrenics part of the way to recovery, which could only make things worse.

At the very least, conventional psychiatry was ignoring the social element in people's difficulties. They were accepting a view of reality which, as he put it, "sanctions a massive ignorance of the social context within which the person was interacting". Maybe their family had made sanity impossible, as his own upbringing had done to him. Maybe the society where they were living before the crisis had caught them in the same kind of mental games and contradictions which had sent them over the edge. Part of the solution then would have to be healing society around the patient, rather than simply fitting them back into a crazy world.

This was the background to his research that led

to the book *Sanity, Madness and the Family* (1964), co-written with the Glasgow psychiatrist Aaron Esterson. The idea was that they would carry out detailed interviews, not just with schizophrenics but also with their families.

There were huge numbers of interviews carried out with Laing and his team, meeting every Tuesday evening, interrogating the transcripts, sometimes acting them out, until they understood what was going on in the interviews with family members too. They tried to do this as objectively as possible, not interrupting and making sure there was no inference from their own experiences or desires.

The conclusion that there was an extra dimension to their difficulties: in fact, if you only see schizophrenia through lens of neuropathology, then it robs you of understanding the vital social element. Schizophrenics seemed so often to be caught in these mental games which their families played, which made it far more difficult for them to get to grips with reality, and suggested that this mental anguish can have biochemical effects.

In other words, Laing and Esterson suggested that signs of schizophrenia may be the result of long-term anxiety and confusion, not the other way around. It was an important blow against those who believed this was all about genetic or chemical imbalances. The book never idealised madness.

They also did control interviews with ordinary healthy families, and were disappointed to find that exactly the same double binds, paradoxes and mental games were used there too – but often more so in the families hit by schizophrenia. Perhaps there was some pre-disposition to mental illness which some people have. Perhaps it was just the sheer intensity of the mental games that made things so difficult among schizophrenics.

Unfortunately, growing rifts between Laing and Esterson meant that the research on healthy families was never published. His critics suggested that this may have been because it would have forced him to face up to some genetic predisposition to mental illness, which he was disinclined to do.

Either way, these ideas put Laing on collision course with the mainstream medical profession. For generations, alternative practitioners have come forward with similar ideas about health – that some symptoms are playing a healing role. From homeopathy to acupuncture, the alternative approach is often about helping the mind or body to heal itself rather than simply suppressing the symptoms of healing. That would shift medical practice from intervening towards some form of accompanying, or maybe mentoring, with their patients. There were, and are, professionals who believe that kind of approach is not just wrong, it also undermines their authority and power.

These issues are especially controversial when it comes to psychiatric disturbances, which you can't see under a microscope and are often just lists of phenomena that tend to go together. Laing's existential approach was that everyone's healing process was different. You had to be with them and let them get on with it, as far as possible. You had to be open to extremely subtle shifts and to notice them, and go with them. It was as much about intuition as it was about formal training.

It was also extremely difficult. Some of the behaviour of his patients was manifestly impossible. But the echoes of the success of the Rumpus Room remained with him and he was determined, with his fellow-conspirators, to do something similar on a grander and more permanent scale. That was the purpose behind the Philadelphia Association, formed with his new allies – the radical psychiatrists – in 1965.

For the past three years, David Cooper had been experimenting with giving his patients more autonomy at Shenley Hospital in St Albans. His centre was called Villa 21 and now the model was used for a major experiment, known to history as

Kingsley Hall.

It so happened that a huge and largely unused building was available next to Bromley-by-Bow underground station in East London. It already had a reputation among radical thinkers. It had been run as a centre along the lines set out by the Russian pioneer of civil disobedience, Leo Tolstoy, and opened by a follower of his called Muriel Lester before the First World War. It had been called after her brother Kingsley (their father had been an admirer of the novelist Charles Kingsley). Gandhi had stayed there on his visit to London in 1931, when he had brought a goat with him to provide him with ultra-local milk. By the spring of 1965, it was largely disused, though still in action as an occasional centre for non-alcoholic drinking and games.

Laing went to see Muriel Lester where she lived in north London, explaining the brutality with which people were treated when they were insane, and the scandal of lobotomies and ECGs against their will. He explained that psychotherapy was only available for people who could pay.

She agreed they could have the building for £1 a year for five years, on condition that it stayed open for the black Christian group who used it for services on Sunday mornings. In fact, Laing fulfilled his promise to preach from their pulpit.

The Philadelphia Association opened Kingsley Hall as a new therapeutic community and began to take referrals for people with schizophrenia or in various stages of mental breakdown. It would be a Rumpus Room writ large, somewhere to go as a refuge to get through the mental healing process. They could scream as loudly as they wanted.

Kingsley Hall became something of a caricature of itself. There was no research, little progress recorded under academic conditions, and few rules. Laing and his colleagues wanted to dispense with formal roles so that it might help people find their authentic rhythms. Cooking and cleaning was done badly, when it was done at all. There were yoga sessions in the morning but otherwise little organisation.

There were also divisions among the Philadelphia Association members about how it should be run. David Cooper was veering in favour of the radical overthrow of imperialism, of which psychiatry was itself a symptom. Laing's co-author Aaron Esterson was on the side of clear demarcation lines and firm ground rules to give stability. The social worker Sidney Briskin actually kept the place running.

Some of those living there became notorious in their own right. There was a middle-aged Catholic nurse who demanded 24-hour therapy, and regressed to infancy for three exhausting years.

There was envy among the other inmates, and her recovery and story remain well-known and controversial to this day. Another resident spent much of the time sitting on the sink dusting his genitals with talcum powder. You could usually see another one walking round at all times armed with a Luger pistol and with a stuffed bird on his head. Laing moved in as well to a flat downstairs with his girlfriend Jutta Werner.

Relations with the local children were especially bad. Kingsley hall residents would see front doors open in the street as they walked by and, one in particular, would just wander in and sit down. There were complaints about very loud record players.

Yet, despite the local suspicion, Kingsley Hall was immensely trendy at the time. Whatever else you might say about it, it wasn't like Netley. Sean Connery even paid a visit. But it only lasted until the lease ran out five years later. It won praise from some of the leading psychologists of the age: D. W. Winnicott, the child development theorist and president of the Psychoanalytical Society, said that he would have liked the chance to do what Laing was doing.

There were no murders and no suicides and nobody who had been there was ever admitted to a mental hospital. But it was also chaotic and possibly dangerous. What really undermined its legacy was that neither Laing nor his colleagues ever followed up the research. They seemed not to have kept the records. Or, if they did, they never wrote them up.

So Kingsley Hall closed, but there were by then other therapeutic communities to carry on with what seemed at the time an important, big idea. There was a huge fundraising event for similar communities in 1971, attended by Michael Caine, John Cleese, Peter Cook and Alan Bennett. Despite the successes, not just by Laing but others all over Europe, it is not an idea which has lasted.

IV

And fall...

"If the human race survives, future men will, I
suspect, look back on our enlightened epoch as a
veritable age of Darkness. They will presumably be
able to savour the irony of the situation with more
amusement than we can extract from it. The laugh's
on us. They will see that what we call
'schizophrenia' was one of the forms in which, often
through quite ordinary people, the light began to
break through the cracks in our all-too-closed
minds."

R. D. Laing, *The Politics of Experience*

By the time Kingsley Hall closed, the world of the
questioning and gently tolerant mid-1960s had run
headlong into the student revolt, the inner city riots
in America, the Paris uprising and the brutalities of
the Vietnam War, from Agent Orange to the My Lai
Massacre.

Laing was in a good position to influence the

mood and increasing numbers, on the Left in particular, were looking to him for answers. Laing himself was allowing his critique of society to reach out further and further from psychiatry. Perhaps because of his upbringing, perhaps because of his need to tell uncomfortable truths – and the background of Lyndon Johnson picking targets for US bombers from the White House – gave Laing a reason and an audience for articulating what he saw as the intense misery of human life, For Laing, we had all become compromised by our social relations and our complicity in the state of the world.

"We are all murderers or prostitutes," he said in his 1967 book *The Politics of Experience*. He rejected conventional political labels, but his approach chimed in with the philosophy of the New Left at the time, which looked to Reich, Fanon, Chomsky, McLuhan, or Marcuse and his critique of a one-dimensional life. That same year, Laing appeared at the Roundhouse in Camden at the 'Dialectics of Liberation' conference, alongside Marcuse himself, plus the poet Allen Ginsberg and the anarchist thinker Paul Goodman – and the Black Power leader Stokely Carmichael.

Laing's critique seemed almost overwhelming. This was, after all, a period when cultural critics accused those around them of denial. The world lived on the brink of nuclear apocalypse, the free world was incinerating the jungles of South East Asia with napalm, and there was certainly a sense in which ordinary life required an element of pretence. It had to, just to get by. "Beauty is almost no longer possible if it is not a lie," he said in *The Politics of Experience*.

Even President Nixon was said to have a copy of it under his pillow, though whether because he thought it was inspiring or because it was a way of better knowing the enemy was not clear. Laing's point of view was that we had been sleep-walking, disconnected with real life, real emotions and real horror.

"I consider many adults (including myself) are or have been, more or less, in a hypnotic trance, induced in early infancy," he wrote in *Politics and the Family* (1969). "We remain in this state until, when we dead awaken – as Ibsen makes one of his characters say – we shall find that we have never lived."

This was Laing's true interest, and as the turmoil of the 1970s began to take shape, the civil rights movement and then civil unrest in Northern Ireland and the looming war in the Middle East, Laing turned increasingly away from formal politics, and was searching for answers to the human crisis primarily inside. "Politically, I think I am neutral really," he said in an interview in 1972, before heading to India on the equivalent of the hippy trail. For Laing, the crisis was as much spiritual and moral as it was political and he was still searching, deeper and deeper.

He went to India that same year and came back desperate to understand these inner truths. He studied with ascetics. He carried on his experiments with LSD. He seemed close to violence himself, as if it was a reality he could not quite side-step. The spirit of the age suggested that violence was a kind of honest response. Certainly Laing used to explode with anger at his lectures and his tours of the USA. He could not stand anything inauthentic or conventional. It enraged him.

He had a complete lack of interest in any kind of small talk or going through the social motions. Even when forced on a lecture tour to fill a sudden hole in his finances, now he was supporting two large families, he would sometimes sit in silence in front of audiences waiting for them to react. Sometimes they did; sometimes they didn't. Sometimes they just complained.

He was by now living partly on the reputation of an *avant garde* thinker, and based partly on the widespread success of his books *The Politics of*

Experience and *The Bird of Paradise*, published as one volume by Penguin. The latter was a somewhat obscure meditation, the former a selection of recent essays, and taken together they appear to be an attempt to delve into the great mysteries of the age. This was a period when the nature of mankind was much debated, based on the latest discoveries of anthropology and archaeology and the possibilities of 'killer apes'.

As Laing pointed out, the previous century had seen the human race killing over 100 million of each other. Like other *platonists*, Laing demonstrated a commitment to the truth and he believed that our collective failure to embrace the truth in all its awkwardness was one of the causes of the violent state of the world. It was one explanation for the madness around us – the lies we tell each other and especially the lies we tell ourselves.

Like his famous American contemporary Ivan Illich, the former Roman Catholic priest turned institutional critic, Laing was interpreting the world as almost the precise opposite of what it seemed to be. Laing's contribution was the idea that we could not bear to see the threat of thermonuclear war hanging over us as it really was, so we dismissed it – and told ourselves reassuring doctrines about the safety of the nuclear umbrella. We live in an exploitative economy with institutions and professions that exploit us, but we have to regard it as benevolence. We make ourselves stupid and organise institutions to make our children stupid too. "Children are not yet fools, but we shall turn them into imbeciles like ourselves, with high IQs if possible," he wrote. That telltale swipe at the one-dimensional IQ figures we used to delude ourselves with was classic Laing. We will return to that theme later – as he did.

We have, in short, an endless capacity to deceive ourselves – and especially somehow by transforming the clear sight of children into the world-weary adults, only half alive, existing in the boardrooms and rat race, that the 1970s radicals so condemned. Again, Laing was identifying the insanity of transforming complex human truth into one-dimensional numbers. It was to become an important theme in his final years.

Timothy Leary, then a spokesperson for the LSD generation, knew Laing by then and described him as a "bridgebuilder between worlds", and that was the sense that Laing managed – deliberately or not – to convey, that he could somehow see another world of truth and harmony behind the veil. That he could see, albeit dimly, some of the answers that eluded the world, if only he could communicate them. But often what he actually communicated was famously obscure. Laing's final words in his book *The Bird of Paradise* were printed on T-shirts across the campuses of the USA. "If I could turn you on, if I could drive you out of your wretched mind, if I could tell you, I would let you know."

There was a sense in which he *could* tell us and let us know, but that it was very hard and we would have to concentrate very hard – as he would – to find these elusive truths. In the meantime, the counterculture – for that was who he was now speaking to and for – would just have to turn themselves on and drive themselves out of their wretched minds. It was poetic and it was meant to be.

Laing believed that poetry might be one way in which he could communicate some of the mental conundrums that catapulted people into mental illness through poetry. His book *Knots* (1970) would include many of them. But there were huge pressures on him to provide answers, to be wise, to spread his love more widely. It was intense and not altogether welcome.

This business of the poetic conundrum, set clearly on the page, also spoke to the spirit of the age, with its transactional analysis and Eric Berne's bestseller *Games People Play*. And Laing was one of the first to articulate the mental damage these games do to us, preventing us from becoming more truly ourselves. This was what he called the 'principle of life in many families' and he set it out in stark clarity in the Massey Lectures in 1968:

"Rule A: don't.
Rule A1: Rule A does not exist.
Rule A2: do not discuss the existence of rules A, A1 and A2."

There in a stark nutshell was the game which drove people insane, as Laing saw it. He had travelled some way intellectually over the previous decade, from complaining about the standardisation and inhumanity of psychiatric treatment to identifying the roots of mental collapse in the alienation of humanity, and the terrible demands that result on some people, reinforced sometimes by their families.

Those same psychic pressures, and the knots in particular, might press down in normal families too – but, as he implied in *Sanity, Madness and the Family*, schizophrenics might also have been people who were, for whatever reason, unable to cope with the intense strain.

The trouble was that this intense strain was taking its toll on Laing as well, and on his relationships with his closest friends. He was drinking heavily, occasionally getting into fights, extricating himself from the extremes of some of his followers. As he struggled to communicate his way of thinking, it was clear that he was also irritatingly and frustratingly misunderstood. "Should we try to get in touch with our feelings now or wait until we graduate," he was asked by one engineering student. It was tough and, over time, it was also debilitating and exhausting.

As the early 1970s turned into the mid-1970s, and the hippies disappeared, the bombing of Cambodia intensified and the threat of Irish and Palestinian terrorists began to take the place of other worries, the sense of a human crisis deepened. War in the Middle East led directly to the Energy Crisis: oil quadrupled in price in a few months, leading to high inflation in the developed nations.

There were real questions abroad about whether civilisation could survive the shock. Private armies emerged in the UK, led by retired generals and SAS founder David Stirling. Bearded, armed survivalists headed to the hills in the USA. Forward-looking people stocked up on grain and tins ready for the coming chaos. The UK government declared a string of states of emergency in quick succession, ending with a period when business was only allowed to work three days in every week. The Red Army Faction emerged in Germany, the Red Brigade in Britain, and the so-called Symbionese Liberation Army kidnapped a wealthy heiress in California and fought to the death with police.

It was the era when people flocked to the emerging new class of guru. Fritz Schumacher's *Small is Beautiful* was a 1973 bestseller and pointed the way towards a new economics, Ivan Illich's critiques of the medical professions (*Limits to Medicine*, 1976) and education (*Deschooling Society*, 1971) were on everyone's bookshelf. It was hardly surprising that people began to talk about living self-sufficiently and buying books that told you how to keep pigs and slaughter them.

Laing married Jutta in February 1974, immediately after the general election which catapulted Ted Heath from power. At the same time, as he discovered later, his mother was at home sticking pins in his effigy, hoping to give him a heart attack. When he brought this up with her in her flat in Glasgow, she said – as she did about so many things – "we don't talk about that kind of thing". It was another 'knot'.

Laing was facing his own particular crisis. In

1975, his daughter Susie got a rare form of leukaemia. Against the advice of nearly everyone – her fiancé, the doctors and her siblings – Laing insisted on telling her the truth that she was going to die. Her response was to discharge herself from hospital and she was able to die at home with some dignity. Then as now, the medical establishment resisted the idea of telling people the full truth about themselves – and especially when they were going to die.

In fact, Illich's book *Limits to Medicine* argued that doctors were actually more frightened of dying than the population they were treating. They were carriers of what he called "infectious fright". The powerful searchlight of the 1970s critique of institutions and professions was now swinging in Laing's direction. The Israeli doctors' strike in 1973 led to a reduction in deaths during the period. Nobody has ever really explained this statistical peculiarity, but Illich and Laing in their different ways were providing some clues.

Then his eldest daughter Fiona had a schizophrenic breakdown herself, Jutta had an affair and Laing retaliated. The incident led to accusations inside the Philadelphia Association that he had slept with one of his patients. Resignations followed and the organisation divided in two. It shouldn't have happened, and particularly not in an organisation dedicated to sanity – but it did.

Laing's drinking became worse. He would insult audiences, especially in the USA, desperately trying to find a way to reveal himself in a way that could be transformative. It was as if, single-handedly, Laing was determined to heal the world.

There were a series of incidents, including the story – perhaps apocryphal – in the home of a potential funder where he challenged his host to a spiritual joust, with the winner to take the daughter of the house. At three in the morning, he declared himself the winner and took the funder's daughter to the bedroom, under the gaze of her enraged boyfriend.

In 1976, his former friend Clancy Sigal, the American writer and former lover of Doris Lessing, published a novel called *Zone of Interior* where Laing was fictionalised into a recognisable caricature called Dr Willie Last. It was bitter and difficult to accept. Kingsley Hall emerged in the novel too as 'Meditation Manor'.

His book sales were going down through most of the 1970s. He tried to launch a range of new projects to provide him with the money he needed to survive. An album of his poems called *Life Before Death* did not work. Nor did his musical show based on his book *Do You Love Me?* He wrote an advice column in *Cosmopolitan* magazine. There were mass rebirthing sessions in the London Hilton. He was becoming increasingly interested in religion. His proposal for an organisation called St Oran's Trust, running urban residential centres for people in distress, came to nothing.

Other books emerged, but his second marriage was unravelling and he was less in the public eye, and less in demand. When the radio psychiatrist Dr Anthony Clare interviewed him in his influential programme *In the Psychiatrist's Chair* in 1983, he admitted to depression for about the past ten years, and alcoholism: yet you could also hear humour and twinkle in his voice. He also asked Laing if he was maybe too sensitive to be a doctor. He replied:

> "I haven't been able to do what most doctors are able to do ... to keep their sensitivity within in fairly ordered frame of conduct, I got tossed and turned."

By then, the spirit of the age had changed. Society had stared into the abyss and turned to the economic conservatives. Margaret Thatcher and Ronald Reagan were in power, intellectually powered by Milton Friedman's monetarist doctrines – and, in many ways, they worked. The new heroes were not psychiatrists, they were business chief executives. A new consensus was emerging on both sides of the Atlantic that the future demanded we should knuckle down and accept what the economy told us. It was a strange rebirth of one-dimensional thinking, where the bottom line seemed for a while to contain the only truth worth knowing.

Then, in 1984 – during the disastrous Miners' Strike – Laing had a child with the therapist Sue Sunkel. Three days after the birth, he was arrested for throwing a bottle through the window of the Bhagwan Rajneesh Centre in Swiss Cottage, around the corner from where he lived in Eton Road. When he was arrested, the police found a small amount of cannabis in his pocket. By the skin of his teeth, he got a conditional discharge and the following month moved in with his secretary Marguerite Romayne-Kendon, a yoga teacher and translator from New Zealand. They never married but she became the mother of his tenth and last child, Charles.

His friend Fritjof Capra, the radical physicist who wrote *The Turning Point* (1982), was told by Laing once that "mystics and schizophrenics find themselves in the same ocean, but the mystics swim whereas the schizophrenics drown."

It did seem in the mid-1980s that Laing was

actually a mystic who was also drowning. Both his grandfather and his father had experienced some kind of mental collapse in their mid-fifties and Laing always expected to do the same. At this point in his life, with his drunken rages and spectacular fallings-out with friends, it looked as though he was doing so.

It was as if he was still taking on the misery of the world too fully, furious also that his career appeared becalmed and jealous of his rival gurus – hence the bottle attack on Bhagwan Rajneesh. His estranged friend David Cooper, author of *Death of the Family*, died in 1986. Laing did not go to the funeral.

V
And rise

"When I entered prison for the first time, I was a medical student. I struggled against fascism and was jailed. I remember the shocking situation that I found myself living. It was the time when the buckets were brought out by the various cells. There was a terrible smell, the smell of death. I remember having the feeling of being in a room where they dissect cadavers. Four or five years after graduation, I became director of a mental hospital, and when I went there for the first time, I felt that same sensation. There was the smell of shit, but there was a symbolic smell of shit. I found myself in a similar situation, a firm intention to destroy that institution. It was not a personal issue. It was the certainty that the institution was completely absurd, only serving the psychiatrists who worked there to earn a salary at the end of the month."
Franco Basaglia, 1979

By 1988, Ronald Laing had ten children and two failed marriages, and was finding that the world had changed around him. Against all expectations, the global economy appeared to be recovering, even if it was on the back of an orgy of speculation and staggering amounts of unrepayable debt. The western world was luxuriating in a sense of triumphalism, especially those in the property market. Accepted opinion had moved away from the platonism of the 1960s.

Ten years after the Energy Crisis, people were turning away from the utopian hopes of the previous decade. It seemed too difficult, too fraught with driving people out of their wretched minds. They wanted security, simple one-dimensional reassurance and obvious objectives. There was no parallel world of reality that meant anything to the new age: this was all there was. The only authentic elements of life were those which could have a price affixed.

In the world of the mind, instead of psychotherapy – with its open-ended commitment – people began to look for more reliable fixes, from Neuro-Linguistic Programming to Cognitive Behavioural Therapy. There may have been a shift engineered in behaviour but there was no underlying shift in consciousness. It seemed safer somehow and, if it was avoiding the unconscionable violence at the heart of real life, then really – who was going to complain. At the same time, the notorious mental hospitals were closing.

This was done partly for humanitarian reasons and partly for economic ones, and it followed the lead taken by Italy under the influence of Laing's famous contemporary Franco Basaglia, who famously shaped Italy's Law 180, which closed their asylums in 1978. Basaglia stayed within the system and arguably had more immediate effect than Laing.

But closing mental hospitals led to another kind of cruelty. Those who had been locked away by society for half a century or more – maybe for something anodyne like sexual liberty or masturbation – were flung back into the community where they had no skills, no networks and no support. And no companionship, which was the vital element in recovery that Laing identified.

But if Laing's own star had been waning, and the genre of psychological games had been replaced in the bookshelves by the new management gurus, and if the hippies and radical utopians had given way to the yuppies – his enemies in the medical establishment did not let up.

During his interview on the radio with Anthony Clare, when Laing admitted that he had problems with alcohol, it happened to coincide with a patient complaining to the General Medical Council that Laing had twice been drunk when giving him a consultation. The GMC used this as an excuse to remove him from the Medical Register, and they used the admission during the radio interview as supporting evidence. The medical bureaucracy ground away relentlessly and they only agreed, finally, to drop the action if he would resign voluntarily from the Register. Planning to return at some point, Laing agreed and was suddenly no longer a medical practitioner.

It was a traumatic period. After his mother died in 1987, he said later that his main regret in life was that he hadn't hurt her more. Yet his resignation from the medical profession at that time also marked a moment in his career when he could begin to be more definitive about what he believed. Despite David Cooper, and despite what he may have said that implied the contrary, Laing never really believed that mental illness was all the fault of patients' families. The phrase 'anti-psychiatry' had hung like an albatross around his neck. It was time to look back over a tumultuous career and be clearer.

He had mellowed in some respects. He had come to believe that the emergence of medical administrators and technocrats was in some ways inevitable. He had always believed that psychiatry could play a useful role looking after people who couldn't look after themselves, doing things that the rest of society could not imagine doing. The key to Laing's approach was always to treat patients like human beings. Back in Netley, he had realised he wouldn't flick the switch to fill their brains with a powerful electrical current if their roles were reversed, so he had stopped doing it. Instead, he did what he believed was right and ignored the consequences – he asked difficult questions, confronted intractable truths.

One story from the end of his career will have to stand for many, described in detail in John Clay's biography *R. D. Laing: A Divided Self*. He was speaking at a major psychology conference in Arizona in 1985, and agreed to go out on the streets to find a woman with paranoid schizophrenia and interview her on film. It was a tremendous conversation and, to everyone's surprise, the woman asked to come on the stage afterwards and gave a calm and intelligent live interview in front of thousands of delegates. It was one of many transformative encounters with Laing.

He asked one aggressive interviewer to have the "humility to admit that he didn't know anything about the sort of process that was going on."

Laing also remained an existentialist. He still believed that psychotic episodes were often a stage on the way to rejecting a false self, to integrating a personality and making it possible to live a more authentic life. He believed his role as a psychiatrist was to facilitate it, not to stop it in its tracks, and to free people from the constraints that psychiatry puts on some irrational behaviour. "Madness need not be all breakdown. It may also be breakthrough," he wrote.

That understanding is still not widespread, and doesn't normally get applied to schizophrenia, but it has lasted – particularly in areas of mental health like family therapy. It came from Laing's forensic interrogation of psychiatry in practice, but it also came from his extraordinary empathy with people in mental distress – which went hand in hand with his weakness, his impatience with conventional thinking and conventional dullness.

It was those early professional years of fearless questioning and experimentation, in the fiercest corners of psychiatric convention like Netley and Catterick, that were – in some ways – the finest moments of Ronald Laing. That becomes clear in one of his last books, the autobiography of those years, his life up to the publication of *A Divided Self*. It's title *Wisdom, Madness and Folly* seems to have been a deliberate echo of Carl Jung's famous memoir *Memories, Dreams, Reflections*, and it allowed him to confront some of the fantasies he had allowed to grow up around him.

He had never glorified schizophrenia, he said. He had never said that there was anything about it that was not painful and that it was often degrading and dehumanising. Schizophrenia was a "hellish world of horror," he said.

The point wasn't that schizophrenics aren't suffering, it is that they remain human when they do so. "I have just said that schizophrenics are as human as we are, just ordinary people who fall apart for one reason or another," he said.

The book was as different from the obscurity of *The Bird of Paradise* as it was possible to be. It was a model of clarity about a heroic period of questioning and a tribute to Laing's greatness.

Towards the end of his life, he gave up alcohol. His partner Marguerite insisted and threatened to leave him if he didn't. It was also clear that he had cancer. He also suffered two minor heart attacks and experienced a near-death experience where he felt he was moving upwards towards the light.

He died of a heart attack while playing a vigorous

game of tennis with friends near St Tropez in 1989. "What fucking doctor?" he said, when they asked him if they could call one. They were his last words. Obscure and cross to the last. He was only 61.

VI
Taking stock

"The Angel that presided o'er my birth Said,
'Little creature, form'd of Joy and Mirth,
'Go love without the help of any Thing on Earth'."
William Blake

Laing set out the core of what he believed in the preface to his 1964 co-written book *Sanity, Madness and the Family*:

> "We do not accept 'schizophrenia' as being a biochemical, neurophysiological, psychological fact, and we regard it as a palpable error, in the present state of the evidence, to take it to be a fact. Nor do we assume its existence, nor do we adopt it as a hypothesis. We propose no model for it."

This didn't mean, as he explained later, that it wasn't real, or that it somehow didn't matter. It certainly didn't mean that it was some kind of Elysian transformation. It hurt. It involved suffering. The point he was making here was that it was not necessarily one, discrete phenomenon, with boundaries and neat scientific definitions. It involved the breakdown of the self, but for multiple reasons and maybe in multiple ways. Laing was denying a single definition, to be treated in a single way.

Laing's was a platonist approach, which spread in the thrilling ferment of the time to medicine, education and beyond – that we carried the seeds of sanity, or health or wisdom, within us and the task of a professional was to help us draw it out. But the utopian spirit of the mid-1970s was not to last. The age to come would reject ideas like this, and was to steamroller over existential psychiatry, complementary health and alternative education.

That may have been inevitable. Because, for all its talk about education being about lighting fires inside, or about drawing out the symptoms of disease, there was a reaction against trendy 'child-centred' education or 'alternative' medicine because the existential approach seemed in practice to frustrate the possibility of change. It seemed to accept too readily people's poor behaviour, their insanity or their disease, or the educational limits of their social background, as if it was reflecting an inner change that never seemed to quiet manifest itself in the outer world. It seemed to be all *breakdown* without a glimmer of *breakthrough*.

That was never Laing's fault, or his responsibility, and it takes in elements of professional life which he never included in his critique. But it was the fault of too many less than inspirational teachers or health practitioners that they forgot the purpose was supposed to be change. Without realising that breakthrough was the name of the game, they got stuck just publicly understanding the symptoms of breakdown. The result, in education at least, was a serious decline in standards, and a backlash against 'modern' teaching methods – and incessant exams and testing against a narrow curriculum, mainly to keep teachers on the correct focus.

When the first school league tables were published in 1992, one headteacher of an unsuccessful secondary school in Leeds, where only two pupils had managed to scrape together five GCSEs, complained to the newspapers: "We have a dreadful problem with truancy and discipline. We have intrusions like motorbikes being ridden into school during the day while lessons are being taught." The problem was that the platonic, existentialist approach to schooling became associated with this kind of failure.

One of the lasting effects of the ferment of debate in the 1970s is that *change*, its possibilities and likelihood and paradoxes, are the key concern of the generation that followed, whether it is personally or politically. It is a criticism of those who followed Laing in his existentialist crusade that they didn't emphasise the vital importance of change enough. You could not just wait forever to make sure that any change was sufficiently 'authentic'. It was the possibility of change that people craved. They still do.

Laing's challenges remain as powerful as ever, and particularly to the professionals. The critique he pioneered against the psychiatric profession was taken up by others against architects, social workers, bankers, journalists, members of Parliament. One by one since then, they have been revealed as operating some kind of conspiracy against the public. Yet the forensic questions raised in the early 1970s by Laing and Illich still have not been faced, let alone answered.

And his influence has been felt in mental treatment, the day centres and support groups which spread out in the wake of his career. It was felt also in community politics. John McKnight, the American pioneer of Asset-Based Community Development, which provided training to Barack Obama in his youth, clearly borrowed from an understanding which derived partly from Laing. This is how McKnight put it:

> "It is the people, caught in this web of counterproductive systems who must seek survival in the hopeless spaces available. They react in many ways, just as we would. They strike out, in anger, just as some of us would. They create productive, phoenix-like new ventures and initiatives, as some of us would. They despair and retreat into addictions as some of us would. They are normal people in an abnormal world, surrounded by expensive, costly helping systems that are the walls that bound their lives. To defy those walls, they must live abnormal lives – often productive, sometimes destructive, always creative."

But despite this influence, Laing's global reputation has not survived him. It never really survived the change of tone at the end of the 1970s. That is not fair, because he saw things – and questioned things – that need to be seen and questioned, and there are still important lessons we can learn from his questions.

There is at least a broad consensus about what he got wrong. The psychotherapist Joseph Berke set these out after his death in the *British Journal of Psychotherapy*. Berke had been closely involved with the patients at Kingsley Hall and now he listed those elements of the story of psychiatry where Laing had blinded himself.

1. He tended to idealise the patient, and to overlook the damage mental patients do to their families and those around them. This is the criticism that Laing was *too* patient-centred. He was too prepared to blame families and forget the devastation that mental distress causes to those around them.

2. He tended to overlook the damage patients did to him. This is a more difficult accusation to sustain but it may be correct that, by exposing himself so closely and so regularly to mental despair, Laing was brutalised and desensitised in the way he treated others. This was also what Antony Clare may have hinted at.

3. He tended to overlook the damage regression can do. Once again, this is about the breakdown becoming more important, in practice, to those who followed Laing than the breakthrough, and thereby

bringing the whole idea into disrepute.

All these criticisms were influential and are probably now widely accepted. But then that sense which Laing promoted of an authentic life within has also been corroded too. Rightly or wrongly, we no longer believe it in quite the same way. Existentialism has lost some of its appeal in the decades since Laing was setting out his ideas for the first time. We have descended into a less civilised, less subtle age, where we have to be able to count things, or look at them under a microscope, before they can be considered seriously. Or before we can be considered serious people.

This is why Laing continues to be a hero, and it is what he continued to fight until his death. The existential view of the psyche meant that a patient's actions might seem perfectly logical, their behaviour sane from their own point of view. And that would not be a delusion but a vital clue in the process of recovery.

"The standard psychiatric patient is a function of the standard psychiatrist, and the standard psychiatric hospital," wrote Laing, and the implication of the existentialist approach to madness is that everyone's breakdown is going to be different. There is no standard. If you think there is one, you will be pretty useless, or pretty brutal, accompanying any process of recovery.

The idea of the non-existence of standard patients was a phrase of his from 1956, but it carried a resonance in his work right through to the end. Because, above all else, it was *standardisation* that Laing fought against. Every profession has its groupthink which renders outsiders as somehow available as victim, whether they the professionals are journalists, architects or investment bankers – and certainly psychiatrists.

The last few decades have seen the opening up of some of those professions, either painfully in the case of tabloid journalists or more gently with the community architecture movement. Psychiatrists have tended to escape the scrutiny of the outside world. It transpired a few years ago that the psychiatrists in charge of a particularly disastrous case in south London had organised an unauthorised system which prevented patients from talking to them directly. Laing would have seen that for what it was – an attempt to raise their status and lower their stress at the expense of the humanity of their patients.

It was still some way from the days when Laing could find patients given ECT or lobotomised regularly, on the whims of single doctors, without any kind of regard for safety or patient preference, but it wasn't that far away. The problem was the rift between psychiatrists and psychologists, and other purveyors of more holistic talking cures. If you looked at people numerically – either as a system of malfunctioning cells and chemicals or as the sum total of their symptoms analysed by a computer – then their personality, Laing said, begins to "fade from view".

What enraged Laing right to the end was the labelling system of the US health insurance system and the way it listed symptoms and categorised – and for its influence on medicine all over the world. He held in particular contempt the Diagnostic and Statistical Manual of the American Psychiatric Association, known at the time as DSM III, the bible of psychiatrists.

With scorn, he would read out passages at conferences, especially in the USA, to show that – using this kind of statistical approach – almost anyone could be treated for almost anything. Just as the Rosenhan experiment showed back in 1973.

This can be true of a range of chronic medical problems which insurance companies, or the NHS, find hard to categorise and therefore to put a price on. But it is particularly true of psychiatric labels, which can't be confirmed by pathologists and which tend to list bundles of symptoms that tend to happen together, then specifying a title and a standard treatment. Take the list of characteristics that define Asperger's Syndrome, for example, as listed in the 1991 official criteria.

This is a list of six categories, and all six have to be ticked before an Asperger's diagnosis can be given - but they can be ticked for completely different oddities within the categories. And if you look closely at the list, you might feel we are absolutely surrounded by people having trouble with their autistic spectrums.

'Imposition of routines and interests', for example. Or 'lack of desire to interact with peers'. Or 'clumsiness', which will describe many of us. 'Formal, pedantic language', 'peculiar stiff gaze', or 'absorbing interest more rote than meaning'? It describes most of the current cabinet, and certainly many psychiatrists. There is the problem. Modern society demonstrates many of the Asperger's traits - and particularly somehow, the people who rule us - yet we only somehow see them in children. Perhaps that is how Professor Simon Baron-Cohen came to publish the theory that Einstein and Newton both had Asperger's on the grounds that they were obsessive and didn't like small talk. Perhaps it was also why we get bizarre statistics like the ones in

Illinois, which saw autism cases rise by 62,000 per cent in the 1990s.

This approach has peculiar side-effects, and the very reverse of the objective, evidence-based foundations it is supposed to rest on. It means that bundles of particular symptoms are often interpreted according to what is trending – which is as much a sign of what the drugs companies are pushing at the time. So we saw the invention of depression, now a widespread chronic condition, which barely existed as a psychiatric concern before 1980 (in the 1970s, the symptom of choice wasn't depression, it was hyper-tension).

This is the danger of standardising psychiatry. This is what Laing wrote in 1986 in the *Times Literary Supplement*:

"What DSM III seems to be is a comprehensive compendium of thoughts, feelings, experiences, unusual experiences, impulses, actions, conduct, which are deemed undesirable, and should be put a stop to, in our culture. It is so all-inclusive that most items of what all the world over at all times and places were deemed to be ordinary manifestations of ordinary human minds, speech and conduct, are ruled out. We, as we used to take ourselves to be, are to be cultured out, to be replaced by a homogenised creature I can hardly recognise as a human being."

In this respect, Laing's radical spirit continues to this day. He knew what would happen if we standardised people, and tried to encapsulate their individuality with numbers to make them easier to process. If they succumbed, it would lead right back to the blindness that simply lobotomised those they found least convenient, or took them outside for a beating as the regime led to at Netley. If they fought back, they had some chance of retaining the right to redefine themselves and their individuality according to their needs, and according to their inner light.

It is impossible to know what Laing would make of the modern world, if he had lived into his eighties and was still with us. On the one hand, there never was an age that believed as much as ours does that we have the right to define ourselves, to be what we feel we are, to break out of conventional definitions if we want to. On the other hand, there never was an age which was so constrained by numbers, definitions, controls by data – there never was such an Aristotelian blankness about the idea of inner health or inner truth and processes of any kind. What would Laing make of it? Who can tell.

The age of Laing, Marcuse and Fanon and the

others, of hippy revolts and utopian experiments, also gave way in the 1980s to the new age of measurement and economic bottom lines – a single number if ever there was one. It wasn't the market that was the problem, so much as the managerialism and the technocrats which came with it. Laing accepted bureaucracy towards the end of his career as a necessary evil if people were to be supported in a systematic way. But he also saw the dangers.

But this isn't about individualism versus the collective. The period we live in now has been described as individualist, which of course it is. But Laing shared that view of the world. He wrote about and became friends with the existentialist philosopher Jean-Paul Sartre, and he supported Sartre in his argument with Camus. There was no such thing as 'we', said Sartre. For Laing and his closest collaborators, we are all isolated individuals. He used to speak of trying to divest himself of all forms of collective identity. It was the collective categorisation that Laing raged against, especially of those in mental distress.

Laing was never keen on socialisation, as if the source of the original mistake was the socially constructed ideas of mental health and ill-health after all. For Laing, we have to be true to ourselves, to live authentically – and it is our overwhelming need to do so that leads sometimes to apparent insanity. In that respect, Laing would not have been on the side of those who try to put the collective good higher than the individual good. Quite the reverse.

But then, he was no constructivist or postmodernist either. If we were entirely socially constructed, then there would be no means by which we might tell the sane from the insane. He was always intolerant of anything fake. One could hardly be more real than the other and Laing believed above all else in authenticity. He was part of a wave of platonism – of believing in a core of inner truth – which broke and may now be gathering again.

Laing and Sartre both believed that scarcity was the explanation for human alienation. The very concept of alienation was actually coming under attack – what were the existentialists claiming people were alienated from? Could you prove it? Could you measure it or see it under a microscope? Worse, the basis of the new reality in the age where we live now was going to be the market – which would put scarcity at the very heart of existence. It would pretend that prices and brand were somehow the only reality, the only sanity.

Laing flirted with politics but he never committed to it, or to the political Left as some of his colleagues did. He mellowed in his critique as he got older, getting more pragmatic. Nor should anyone assume that this interpretation is a critique of free market economics, which is simply a pragmatic way of organising economics.

Laing didn't live to see the apotheosis of market relations that became so mainstream by the 1990s that every respectable political approach seemed to embrace it. He did not see the way The Market was raised to a kind of untouchable, god-like status. We don't know what he would have said, but we can probably guess.

In fact, the individualism of the age of market economics is anyway delusory. The real damage is not done so much by the market, which is a useful human construct. It is the way that we see *only* the market and nothing behind it. It is a one-dimensional attempt to understand the world in simplistic and dishonest terms. It goes hand in hand with American contract culture. It goes hand in hand with key performance indicators, data, targets and other numerical attempts to reduce human beings to numbers.

Laing's biographer Daniel Burston described him as "an accomplished pianist, a precocious student of the classics, a rebel and a romantic, an iconoclast, psychoanalyst, philosopher, theologian and drunk." He was, of course, much more than that. He was a successful reformer, leading the charge against some of the inhumanity in psychiatric medicine – though only some – a pioneer of the expression of emotion in mainstream mental health services, and a prophet. And like other prophets, he wasn't really honoured as he should have been in his own country.

He may not have been right about everything – who is? But he was still one of the co-creators of the modern world. And the modern world is once again in flux, as it was when he was at the height of his fame. It may be that he provided a clue about how we can find a safe way through.

Find out more

Daniel Burston (1996), *The Wing of Madness: The life and work of R. D. Laing,* Cambridge: Harvard University Press.

John Clay (1996), *R. D. Laing: A divided self,* London: Hodder and Stoughton.

David Cooper (1971), *Death of the Family*, London: Penguin Books.

Edgar Z. Friedenberg (1973), *Laing*: Glasgow, Fontana Modern Masters.

Adrian Laing (1994), *R. D.Laing: A biography*, London: Peter Owen.

R. D. Laing (1965), *A Divided Self,* Harmsansworth: Penguin Books.

R. D. Laing (1967), *The Politics of Experience and the Bird of Paradise,* London: Penguin Books.

R. D. Laing and Aaron Esterson (1970), *Sanity, Madness and the Family: Families of schizophrenics*, London: Pelican Books.

R. D. Laing (1971), *Knots*, London: Penguin Books.

R. D. Laing (1979), *Sonnets,* London: Michael Joseph.

R. D. Laing (1985), *Wisdom, Madness and Folly: The making of a psychiatrist 1927-1957*, London: Macmillan
.

Clancy Sigal (1976), *Zone of the Interior*, New York: Thomas Crowell.

Scandal: How homosexuality became a crime

By the same author.
Also published by The Real Press, available in print and as an ebook (see www.therealpress.co.uk).

It was Saturday 6 April 1895. The weather was windy and drizzly as the passengers packed onto the quayside at Dover to catch the steam packet to Calais, due on the evening tide. Perhaps it was packed that night because of Easter the following week. Perhaps it wasn't as packed as some of the witnesses claimed later, or the downright gossips who weren't actually there. But it was still full. Those waiting on the quay wrapped up warm against the chilly Channel breeze and eyed each other nervously, afraid to meet anyone they knew, desperately wanting to remain anonymous.

Among those heading for France that night was an American, Henry Harland, the editor and co-founder of the notorious quarterly known as *The*

Yellow Book, the journal of avant garde art and writing which had taken England by the scruff of the neck in the 1890s. Harland had come to Europe with his wife Aline, pretending to have been born in St Petersburg and planning to live in Paris, but had instead made his London flat, at 144 Cromwell Road, the very hive of excitement in the literary world. Henry James, Edmund Gosse and Aubrey Beardsley came and went. The parties were talked about with awe and excitement. Henry and Aline always spent the spring in Paris, so they were not leaving the country suddenly and in desperation, but it dawned on them that the reason the quayside was so packed that night was because many others were.

The name of the ferry the Harlands boarded has been lost to history. It was probably the *Victoria* – her sister ship the *Empress* had been badly damaged in a collision the month before and was now in dry dock. There she heaved beside the sea wall, as the muffled passengers filed up the gangway, her twin rakish masts and her twin funnels belching smoke, her two paddlewheels poised to drive across the world's busiest sea lane at 18 knots, her stern flag flapping in the wind with the insignia of the London, Chatham and Dover Railway.

Harland had a good idea why the ferries were full, though he was still surprised. He was also aware of at least some of the implications for himself. Oscar Wilde had been arrested for 'gross indecency' that evening, having lost his libel action the day before. The news of the warrant for his arrest was in the evening papers, and included the information that Wilde had been arrested while he had been reading a copy of *The Yellow Book* (this was quite wrong, in fact; he was reading *Aphrodite* by Pierre Louys). Harland could only guess the motivations of those who were now suddenly crowding across the English Channel, but it looked remarkably like fear. They huddled in corners in the stateroom downstairs, out of the wind, damp and smuts, wondering perhaps whether they would ever see their native land again.

There was an unnerving atmosphere of menace that evening. One item in the evening papers implied that the nation was perched on the edge of a scandal that would make the establishment teeter. "If the rumours which are abroad tonight are proved to be correct we shall have such an exposure as has been unheard of in this country for many years past."

Did it mean the exposure would reach those who run the nation, or did it mean something even more terrifying – that the exposure would spread downwards through society? As the passengers knew only too well, the combination of events which they had feared for a decade had now come to pass. It had been a few months short of ten years since the so-called 'Labouchère amendment' had been rushed through the House of Commons, criminalising homosexual activity of any kind between men. It was never quite clear why women were excluded – there is no evidence for the old story that Queen Victoria claimed it was impossible. For ten years now, they had watched the rising sense of outrage at the very idea of 'homosexuality' – though the term was not yet in common use – and had realised that there might come a time when that law was enforced with an unsurpassed ferocity.

It wasn't that they necessarily had anything to be ashamed of – quite the reverse – but they had reputations to be lived down, some event in their past or some 'unfortunate' relationship behind them. Now that public concern had turned

to what looked like public hysteria, they clearly had to be vigilant. They did not want to be accused, as Oscar Wilde was accused, by a violent aristocrat of doubtful sanity, and would then have to respond in the courts or the press. They could not face the fatal knock on the front door from a smiling acquaintance who would turn out to be a dangerous blackmailer.

But now the unthinkable had happened. Wilde had been stupid enough to sue the Marquess of Queensberry for libel, and had lost. The public had driven each other into a crescendo of rage and it seemed only sensible to lie low in Paris for a while. Or Nice or Dieppe, or the place where the British tended to go in flight from the law – Madrid. Anywhere they could be beyond the reach of the British legal system.

As we shall see, one of those who fled, as I discovered during the research that led to this book, was my own great-great-grandfather – escaping for the second time in a just over a decade, in a story that my own family had suppressed for three generations.

It is no small matter to flee your home and go abroad, especially to do so within the space of a few hours to gather your belongings and make arrangements for your property or your money. As it is, escape was only a solution available to those wealthy enough to flee. It is even tougher perhaps for those in some kind of unconventional relationship, ambiguous to the outside world – but perhaps not ambiguous enough – aware that the decision to go was probably irreversible. It might look like an admission of guilt.

On the other hand, what might happen when the newspapers could unleash this kind of bile? What would happen when they had successfully gaoled Wilde with hard labour and turned on his friends, and anyone else who looked unusual? What would happen if the rumours were correct and the scandal would shortly engulf the government and royal family? Harland did not know at this stage that, when the news about *The Yellow Book* became clear on Monday morning, a mob would gather outside the offices of his publishers Bodley Head, and would break all the windows. "It killed *The Yellow Book* and it nearly killed me," said publisher John Lane later.

We know now that, in the event, the threatened conflagration did not take place, but in the remaining 72 years while Section 11 of the Criminal Law Amendment Act, the Labouchère Amendment, stayed on the statute books, 75,000 were prosecuted under its terms, among them John Gielgud, Lord Montagu and Alan Turing. Many thousands of lives were ruined – Turing committed suicide not long afterwards, having been forced to undergo hormone treatment that made him grow breasts.

Yet that moment of fear in Britain in 1895, unprecedented in modern times, has been largely forgotten. It is remembered as a sniggering remnant of gossip, about the number of English aristocrats or others in public life, living incognito in Dieppe, or glimpsed in the bars in Paris, and the awareness as a result that they had something to hide. One of the purposes of this book is to remember it for what it was – one of the most disturbing chapters in modern English history, when public horror at sexual behaviour reached such intensity that nobody seemed completely safe, and nobody could be relied on to protect you. And when a man like Wilde, the darling of the theatre critics, with two sell-out shows in London's West End theatres, could be brought low by a furious, litigious pugilist – well, really, who was safe?

This unique moment of fear in English history came at a peculiar moment, at perhaps the apogee of tolerance in so many other ways – women were cycling and getting university degrees, training to be doctors. Mohandas Gandhi was a London-trained barrister working in South Africa. George Bernard Shaw was overturning assumptions about the right way to dress, eat and spell. H. G. Wells was sleeping his way through the ranks of the young female Fabians. Edward Carpenter, in his sandals, was advertising freedom from the constraints of conventional sexuality, having forged a gay relationship with a working class man from Sheffield. William Morris was still, just, preaching a revolution based on medieval arts and crafts. And yet the rage at the idea that men should love each other sexually threatened to overwhelm everything.

That morning, Queensberry had received a telegram from an anonymous supporter, which read: "Every man in the City is with you. Kill the bugger."

Why did it happen? Partly because of growing public concern following the Labouchère amendment, sneaked though Parliament in 1885, but even that was more than the individual brainchild of a lone radical. Why this shift from tolerance of the changing role of women and emerging new ideas to this threatening public rage? How did homosexuality emerge as a key issue in English public life?

The answer lies in the events that took place in Dublin a decade before, starting with the political aftermath of the murder of Lord Frederick Cavendish, the son of the Duke of Devonshire and the newly-appointed Chief Secretary to Ireland.

But I had a more personal reason for finding out the answers to some of these questions. My family lived in Dublin in the 1880s. The reason that they don't any more, and that I was born in England not Ireland, was because of those same events there in that decade. Until the last few years, when I began researching this book, I was unaware of them.

All I knew was that my great-great-grandfather, the banker Richard Boyle, had left Dublin suddenly and under a cloud around 1884. His photograph has been torn out of the family photo album, with only his forehead remaining. There are no likenesses of him anywhere that I know about. The letters related to these events in the family, and what followed, have long since been destroyed. I believe I was even there when my grandfather burned the last of them on the bonfire around 1975.

I had always been interested in what might have happened, but had assumed that the memories were now beyond recovery, just as the fate of my great-great-grandfather was lost in the mists of unfathomable time.

As it turned out, I was wrong. I was working on another incident in Irish history in the British Library, and discovered as I did so that a whole raft of Victorian Irish newspapers had been digitised and were now searchable online. On an impulse, I put in the name 'Richard Boyle' and searched through the references in the Dublin papers. Then, suddenly, my heart began beating a little faster, because there it was – the first clue I found to a personal tragedy, and a national tragedy too: this was the spark that lit the fuse which led to the criminalisation of gay behaviour and the great moment of fear that followed the arrest of Oscar Wilde.

That first clue led to others, which led to others. I will never know the whole story, but what I did discover took me on a historical rollercoaster, and an emotional one, which catapulted me back to the strangely familiar world of the end of the nineteenth century – and a glimpse of that sudden fear in April 1895 that drove many of those affected so suddenly abroad....

Read more by buying Scandal...

Other titles by David Boyle

Building Futures
Funny Money: In search of alternative cash
The Sum of our Discontent
The Tyranny of Numbers
The Money Changers
Authenticity: Brands, Fakes, Spin and the Lust for
Real Life
Blondel's Song
Leaves the World to Darkness (fiction)
Toward the Setting Sun
The New Economics: A Bigger Picture (with
Andrew Simms)
Money Matters: Putting the eco into economics
The Wizard
Eminent Corporations (with Andrew Simms)
Voyages of Discovery
The Human Element
On the Eighth Day, God Created Allotments
The Age to Come
Unheard, Unseen: Submarine E14 and the
Dardanelles
Broke: Who killed the middle classes?
Alan Turing: Unlocking the Enigma
Rupert Brooke: The Last Patriot

Jerusalem: England's National Anthem
Give and Take (with Sarah Bird)
People Powered Prosperity (with Tony Greenham)
Rupert Brooke: England's Last Patriot
How to be English
Operation Primrose
Before Enigma
The Piper (fiction)
Scandal
How to become a freelance writer
V for Victory
Lost at Sea
Regicide (fiction)
The Death of Liberal Democracy?
(with Joe Zammit-Lucia)
Prosperity Parade
Cancelled!
Like leaves fall in Autumn: Hotspur, Henry IV and
the Battle of Shrewsbury

See also our website at www.therealpress.co.uk

www.ingramcontent.com/pod-product-compliance
Lightning Source LLC
Chambersburg PA
CBHW020551030426
42337CB00013B/1041